HARNESSING ENERGY · HARNESSING ENERGY

COAL POWER

BY DIANE BAILEY

CREATIVE ◗ EDUCATION

HARNESSING ENERGY

HARNESSING ENERGY

TABLE OF CONTENTS

PEACE AND WAR. WEALTH AND POVERTY. PROGRESS AND SETBACKS. HISTORY HAS BROUGHT HUGE SWINGS IN THE HUMAN CONDITION, AND WITH EVERY CHOICE PEOPLE MAKE, THERE IS THE POTENTIAL TO MOVE FORWARD OR STEP BACKWARD. AT THE CORE OF THIS CONTINUAL STRUGGLE HAS BEEN THE QUEST FOR ENERGY. ENERGY GAVE HUMANS POWER AND MOTIVATED THEM TO DO GREAT THINGS—WITH BOTH POSITIVE AND NEGATIVE EFFECTS. WITHOUT ENERGY, PEOPLE WOULD NOT BE ABLE TO DRIVE CARS, OPERATE COMPUTERS, OR POWER FACTORIES. WARS ARE FOUGHT TRYING TO DOMINATE SOURCES OF ENERGY. FORTUNES ARE MADE AND LOST DEPENDING ON HOW THAT ENERGY IS MANAGED. THE LAWS OF PHYSICS STATE THAT ENERGY CANNOT BE CREATED OR DESTROYED. THAT IS TRUE, BUT ENERGY CAN BE HARNESSED AND DIRECTED. IT CAN BE WASTED, OR IT CAN BE COAXED INTO EFFICIENCY. CIVILIZATIONS AND TECHNOLOGIES HAVE LEAPED FORWARD—AND SOMETIMES BACKWARD—AS HUMANS HAVE TAPPED INTO EARTH'S SOURCES OF ENERGY.

The coal we use today took millions of years to form.

Coal could be called the granddaddy of the fossil fuels. Societies the world over have used it for thousands of years. It was humans' first introduction to the wealth of energy buried in the earth. As coal became ever-present in daily life, people developed a love-hate relationship with it. Some thought it provided protection against the bubonic plague. Others blamed it for making people cranky and bald—and with bad teeth, to boot. Coal smoke choked the air, and its grimy dust clung to everything, but the reward was that it changed cold into heat and brought light to the dark-ness. Threaded through the earth's crust like ribbons, this humble black rock—lumps of compressed carbon—opened the door to new technologies, new economies, and ultimately, a transformed world.

CHAPTER ONE

A PORTABLE CLIMATE

IT'S HARD TO IMAGINE WHAT HUMANS FIRST THOUGHT OF COAL. It looked like any other rock. But, on further inspection, it turned out to be something much better. Like wood, it *burned*. Inside those black rocks was a reserve of energy, collected some 300 million years ago. Like a genie in a bottle, its energy was just waiting to be released.

Hot and steamy: That was the weather report from the **Carboniferous period**. Conditions were perfect for trees and

The late Carboniferous period featured swamp forests ideal for producing coal.

plants to flourish in the swamps and bogs that covered large portions of the planet. Like all living things, this vegetation consisted mainly of carbon—an element packed with energy. When these plants died, their leaves and branches sank into the water. Sand, mud, water, and rocks buried them. These remains were not exposed to air, so the carbon did not **react** with oxygen to become carbon dioxide. Instead, over time, heat and pressure built up on this plant material. These conditions pressed out any remaining moisture to leave behind slabs of black, carbon-rich material—coal.

Imagine a huge peanut butter and jelly sandwich. That's what coal **seams** look like inside the earth. These seams range from a few inches to many feet thick. There are several different types of coal. Anthracite is the rarest. It is very hard and contains the most carbon. Anthracite is difficult to ignite, but once it catches fire, it burns the hottest of all the types of coal. It produces more heat per pound but makes the least pollution. Next on the scale are bituminous and sub-bituminous coal. Bituminous coal has the higher carbon content of the two, and it burns better. However, sub-bituminous coal has less sulfur, one of coal's most dangerous pollutants. Lignite ranks at the bottom of the coal scale. It has a low carbon content, is softer, and its color is more brown than black.

Unlike other fossil fuels, such as oil, a lot of coal is found closer to the surface of the earth. It's easy to reach, so people have used it for centuries. Scientists have discovered that people living 6,000 years ago, during

Coal seams can be up to 90 feet (27.4 m) thick and 920 miles (1,481 km) long.

the **Stone Age**, used coal to fuel their fires. In ancient China, people used some coal, but they still depended mostly on wood for heat—especially when they were working with metal. Coal contained too many impurities and made too much smoke to be used for making iron. However, by the 11th century, the Chinese had used up too much of their forestland and needed another power source. They figured out that coal could be purified by pre-burning it to remove some of the pollutants. The result was a substance called coke. Coke burned hotter than plain coal and made less smoke. It was much better for operating ironworks.

A similar pattern was followed several centuries later in Europe. In the late 1500s, the population was growing in what is now the United Kingdom (England, Northern Ireland, Scotland, and Wales). As people burned more wood, the supply started shrinking. But coal was everywhere. It was even visible atop the ground and sticking out of seaside cliffs. Britons then turned to coal to fuel their fires. The scenario repeated in the United States in the 1800s. American philosopher Ralph Waldo Emerson observed, "Every basket [of coal] is power and civilization. For coal is a portable climate. It carries the heat of the tropics to Labrador and the polar circle."

For centuries, families the world over carried coal to their homes for heat and light.

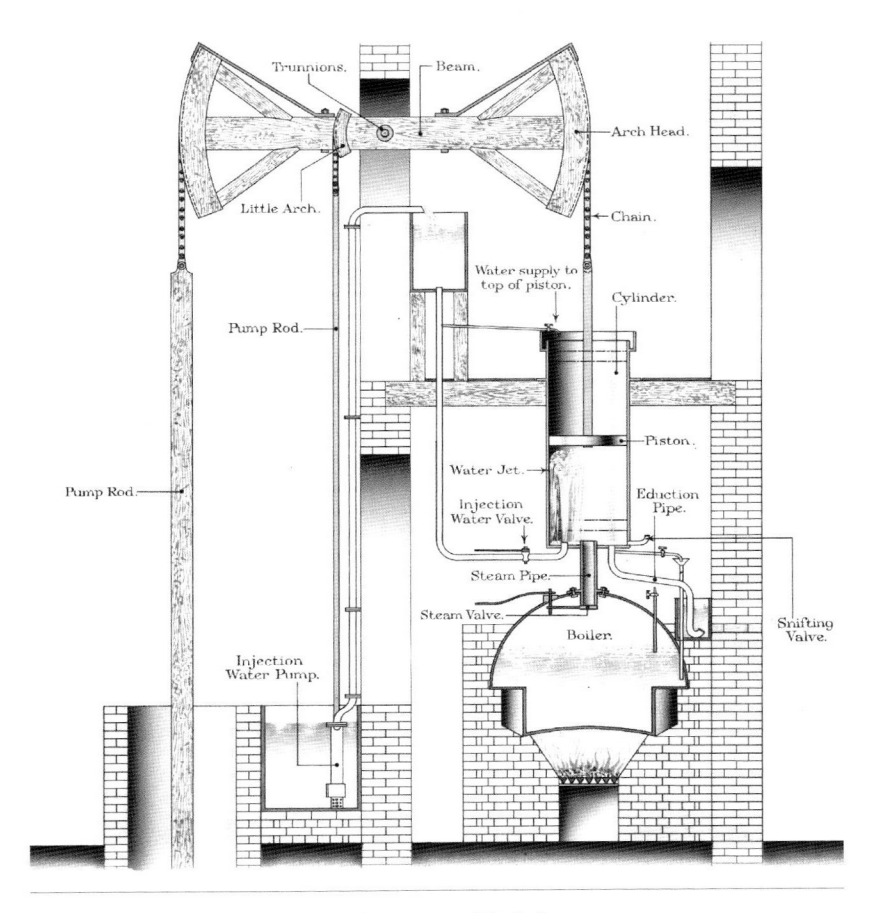

*Newcomen's design enabled the pumping
cycle to repeat 12 times per minute.*

One invention almost single-handedly turned coal from an available fuel source into an entire industry. In 1698, English inventor Thomas Savery built a steam engine and received the first patent for the technology. His design was then refined by another Englishman, Thomas Newcomen. In 1712, Newcomen's steam engine was installed at a coal mine. Mines were vulnerable to flooding, but the steam engine could pump out the water. That made it safer for miners to go underground and allowed them to go deeper than they could before. Not only did the steam engine make mining easier, but the machine itself was powered by coal, and it was made of iron that had been forged over a coal-powered fire. Half a century later, James Watt, a Scottish inventor, improved the design of the steam engine even further. It went on to power the coal industry for two more centuries.

At the turn of the 19th century, the way people lived in Europe and the U.S. started to change. For centuries, most people had lived on farms. They grew their own food. They made their clothes, tools, and other items by hand. But the **Industrial Revolution**, which occurred over several decades, brought huge developments in technology. Machines were built that let workers make things in large volumes. These machines were faster. They were more efficient. And they required a lot more power.

People needed a cheap, reliable, and powerful source of energy. Britons knew that coal had a higher energy content and burned hotter than wood. They started pulling coal out of the hills in massive quantities. Fed by coal, the Industrial Revolution turned the United Kingdom into a dominant world power. The U.S. was not far behind. Pittsburgh, Pennsylvania, was one of America's first manufacturing centers. Workers in the glass and iron industries relied on steam produced from the region's

power-packed anthracite coal. Anthracite was also a natural choice to fuel the growing railroad industry in the 1800s. Meanwhile, scientists used other chemicals from coal tar to manufacture products ranging from pharmaceuticals to paint.

Coal dominated the industrial world by the end of the 1800s. Another development—electricity—made it even more important. American inventor Thomas Edison helped develop the technology to make electricity practical as a source of power. He was also a shrewd businessman who wanted to sell electricity to customers. In 1882, Edison opened a coal-fired electric generating plant in New York and began selling his product. Soon, electricity became the power system of choice. As it did, coal disappeared from homes, since people did not have to haul heavy buckets of coal to light their fires. They did not have to wash black, sooty **residue**

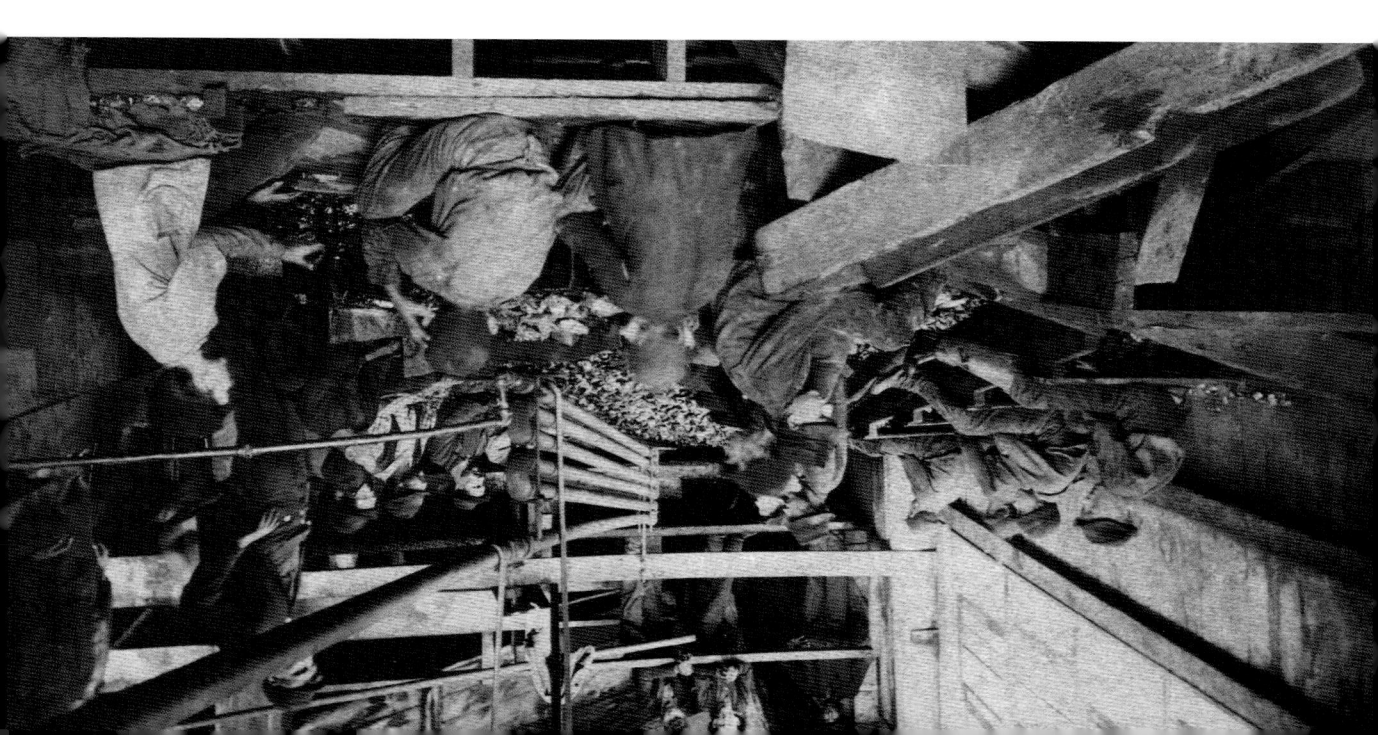

Young *"breaker boys"* in a Pennsylvania mine were tasked with separating coal.

Thomas Edison's Pearl Street Station used coal to run steam-engine generators.

from their clothes and windows. Electricity was clean, easy, and instantaneous. However, coal did not really disappear. Instead, it went into hiding, swallowed by the fires of power plants.

Although coal has been heavily used over the past two centuries, large deposits still remain all around the globe. There are huge amounts of coal in the U.S., Russia, China, India, Australia, Poland, Germany, and South Africa. How much? Estimates range from about 850 to 1,000 billion tons (771–907 billion t). That would be enough to last for more than 100 years.

However, some experts say those numbers are misleading. Recent reports suggest that coal reserves have been overestimated because the figures are often based on outdated **geological** information. Over the last several years, many countries have reported smaller reserves than in the past. One report predicted that coal mining would peak by the year 2025 and then decline, especially after 2050. In addition, the trend is for the best coal to be mined first, leaving behind lower-quality, less energy-dense varieties.

More coal deposits could be discovered to help meet increasing demand. And as technology improves, it may become practical to mine coal that was previously too difficult to reach. However, projections of how long coal will last are often based on how much people are using *now*—not estimates of what they will use in the future. The problem is that people are not using the same amount of power from year to year. Instead, they are using more all the time.

CHAPTER TWO

POWER TO
THE PEOPLE

TO MANY PEOPLE TODAY, COAL MAY SEEM OLD-FASHIONED, THE FUEL OF A PAST ERA. In fact, it's a huge force in today's societies. As Ken Blackwell, a Republican politician from Ohio, wrote in a 2012 article for the American *Spectator:* "Coal today may seem of little relevance … But long after it disappeared from the uses most visible to city dwellers, coal is still the critical fuel behind the everyday functions of their lives." Coal shows up in people's lives in countless ways. The steel in cars was probably forged in a coke-fired plant. The roads on which those cars drive may be sealed with pitch, a waterproof, sticky substance made from a byproduct of coal. Paper, soap, concrete, and fertilizer all use coal byproducts as well. By far, however, the biggest use of coal is in fueling electric power plants.

When coal pitch is heated, it releases chemicals that are dangerous to inhale.

Coal is plentiful and inexpensive, which has helped make electricity widespread. In developing places such as China, India, and Africa, the demand for electricity is still growing. That means the demand for coal is growing, too.

Coal is not the only fuel that can run an electrical power plant. Natural gas, nuclear energy, and hydroelectric power can also do the job. So can **renewable** sources of energy, such as solar or wind. The problem with renewables is in the timing. Electricity cannot be effectively stored, or saved up and used when needed. Instead, a consistent supply of electricity depends on a consistent source of power. If the sun isn't shining or the wind isn't blowing, then people must turn to something more reliable. The wide availability of coal makes it the go-to fuel for much of the world.

Bituminous and sub-bituminous coal make up most of the world's coal resources. They are known as "steam coal," because they fuel electric power plants that use steam. After this coal is mined, it is crushed into small **granules** before being burned in a power plant. This increases its surface area. A handful of coal dust, with more exposed surface than one big lump, can burn faster. The coal is also washed to remove some of the

Electric power plant workers unload, separate, and store coal in large piles.

pollutants, such as sulfur. Then the coal is shoveled into a furnace, where it's burned to heat water into steam. The steam pressure powers a **turbine**, which spins a magnet that produces electricity. Coal fuels about 40 percent of the world's electricity. Some countries, such as South Africa and Poland, make almost all their electricity with coal. The U.S. uses coal for about 40 percent of its overall electrical production, although that figure is expected to drop as natural gas becomes cheaper.

Overall, coal is used for about one-fourth of the world's total energy needs. That includes electricity, heating, and industrial uses. About half of the world's total coal use occurs in China. With its growing population and **infrastructure**, China consumes more than the U.S., Japan, and Europe put together. A new coal-burning power plant goes up in China about every week. India is the world's second-largest user of coal. In 2010 alone, the nation approved enough new coal plants to build one every other day. Coal plants continue to be built in Europe, both to replace aging ones and to increase overall power production. Coal is also seeing a resurgence in Europe due to concerns about the dangers of nuclear power.

To feed these plants, geologists and engineers stay busy looking for new coal deposits and figuring out how to get more coal from hard-to-reach places. Some coal is easy to see—it's right on the surface. Other times,

scientists look for areas that have the right geology for coal formation. Then they drill down and pull up a rock sample to see if it contains coal. Sometimes they don't have to drill. Instead, they use magnetic pulses or **radar** to indicate what materials are buried there.

Coal that's close to the surface can be collected relatively easily. Strip mining is when bulldozers simply "strip" away the soil to get to the coal. In "mountaintop removal," miners use explosives to blast away mountaintops to reach the coal underneath. Both of these approaches are simple, technically. However, they are controversial because they damage the surrounding land. Deeper coal seams are mined by drilling into the earth and then pulling up the coal through shafts or

An underground mine (above) can extend as far as 2,000 feet (610 m) into the earth. Surface mines (below) require large machinery to move layers of dirt.

tunnels. This type of mining is more difficult, expensive, and dangerous to miners.

Coal is a relatively easy fuel to use, but it has one huge downside: it's dirty. Coal is responsible for a tremendous amount of pollution worldwide. Small particles of coal dust are in the air and can be breathed in, causing disease. Chemicals are released when coal burns. They can soak into the soil and re-emerge in food or contaminate the water supply and fall as acid rain. One major pollutant in coal is sulfur, which forms the poisonous gas sulfur dioxide as coal burns. To prevent as much sulfur dioxide from going into the air, coal can be washed before it's burned. After it's burned, chemical "scrubbers" take over. These scrubbers are not fancy brushes. Rather, they are chemicals that bind with the sulfur that's in the smoke, preventing the sulfur from being released into the air. Unfortunately, the technology used for chemical scrubbing is very expensive. It also creates a toxic **sludge** that must be disposed of.

Coal ash is what burning coal leaves behind, and it poses another problem. Some ash can be recycled into useful products, such as concrete. But there's too much to be able to get rid of it all that way. Much of the ash is dumped into landfills. There it can leak toxic chemicals such as lead and arsenic into groundwater. Coal plants also emit, or give off, particles of other toxic materials, such as mercury. Mercury is a highly toxic metal that can cause permanent brain damage and even

Acid rain harms the entire life cycle, from water sources to plants and wildlife.

death, especially in young children. In addition, coal-burning produces several gases, including nitrogen dioxide and nitric oxide, ozone, and carbon dioxide. These **greenhouse gases**, especially carbon dioxide, contribute to the problem of **global warming**.

Several technologies are used to make coal cleaner and more efficient. At a traditional coal-fired plant, the energy efficiency is only about 30 to 35 percent. For years, chemists and physicists have worked to squeeze more power out of coal. One solution is to go beyond steam. Some power plants instead use supercritical water. Water that is below its critical point still has distinct liquid and gas phases. When it is subjected to a higher pressure and temperature, it becomes supercritical, and the two states become indistinguishable from one another. Power plants that use supercritical water are more efficient and can produce the same amount of power using less fuel. China, Denmark, Germany, and Japan are building supercritical and even ultra-supercritical plants, which can boost coal's efficiency to almost 50 percent.

Another technology at work is converting coal into synthetic natural gas, or syngas. This process removes pollutants such as mercury and sulfur. Syngas burns cleaner and produces less carbon dioxide. Gasified coal is also more efficient because it can be used in a two-step system called the Integrated Gasification Combined Cycle (IGCC). During the first step, syngas is burned to power a turbine that generates electricity. As the gas burns, it gives off heat. This heat is channeled to make steam that runs a second turbine, generating more electricity. This technology has environmental benefits, but it is expensive.

No one can argue that coal is perfect, but it's like a fast-food hamburger: although it may not be the best thing for you, it's easy, cheap, and does the job. Coal is not a fuel that will solve energy and environmental problems with one swift blow. But it's likely to still be widely used in the future.

The greenhouse gases contained in the atmosphere absorb the sun's rays and trap heat.

CHAPTER THREE

BURNING THROUGH THE FUTURE

SO FAR, THERE HASN'T BEEN A BIG SURGE IN SOLAR-POWERED COMPUTERS OR WIND-POWERED WASHING MACHINES. But the world's demand for power is growing—and quickly. Worldwide, the U.S. Energy Information Administration estimates that the use of coal will increase almost 50 percent between 2015 and 2035, mostly because of electricity. China and India are the world's two largest countries. Together, they account

In places such as India, constant exposure to coal dust and fumes can lead to lung and skin diseases.

Air pollution enshrouds Shanghai, China, and its 23.5 million inhabitants.

for more than a third of the world's population. Many of their citizens still do not have electricity, but that is changing quickly. U.S. journalist and energy expert Richard Heinberg writes in his book *Blackout*, "Coal is at the center of energy planning for many nations— especially the burgeoning Asian economies."

Coal has long been a huge factor in the battle between the economy and the environment. That keeps scientists busy looking for some kind of truce. The idea of "clean coal" has been around for decades. It has gained more attention as pollution gets worse and laws limiting pollution get tougher. To environmentalists, the idea of "clean coal" is an **oxymoron**. Coal is the filthiest of all the fuels. It can't be *entirely* clean. But it can be cleaner.

Coal is already treated to wash off some poisonous substances. But a huge problem still remains with carbon dioxide. Every year, coal-burning plants pump billions of tons of carbon dioxide into the air. In small amounts, carbon dioxide is not dangerous. But problems arise when there is too much. Forests and oceans are natural carbon sinks, or places that absorb carbon dioxide. They can store some of the carbon dioxide that people make. Unfortunately, humans make it faster than nature can soak it up.

To combat the problem, many experts have suggested "catching" carbon dioxide and then storing it underground. The goal of carbon capture and storage (CCS) has led to the development of several technologies, including the capture of carbon dioxide as coal burns. Chemicals bind to the carbon dioxide as soon as it's released. This makes it possible to separate it from the rest of the exhaust. Once the carbon dioxide is collected, some of it can be used for other industries. For example, it can be pumped underground into old oil deposits, where it mixes with the oil and loosens it enough that it can be pumped to the surface. Such operations are in force in Texas and the Canadian province of Saskatchewan. Carbon dioxide can also be buried underground, but that's tricky. Such sites require a certain set of geological criteria to make sure the carbon dioxide doesn't leak. Also, while several million tons of carbon dioxide are stored underground today, that is not an efficient solution, and the figure represents less than one percent of how much is produced.

Germany was home to the world's first power plant to use carbon dioxide separation via CCS technology.

Lack of support and legal trouble led energy company Vattenfall to cancel a German CCS project in 2011.

Although CCS technology shows promise, it's complicated and expensive. Only a few demonstration projects are scattered worldwide. In 2011, two major projects were canceled in Scotland and Germany, setting back the industry. Natural gas also threatens some of these projects, because it is cleaner than coal and competitive in price. In some cases, it's easier to just switch over. However, CCS projects will likely gain some ground as the need for coal continues to clash with environmental worries.

People may be hungry for coal, but coal itself is thirsty for water. Coal plants need tremendous amounts of water to cool them down, and that could affect how much they are used in the future. In 2012, a team of scientists in the U.S. and Europe predicted that lower water levels, resulting from droughts and warmer temperatures, would force occasional shutdowns of coal-powered plants. That could result in a 4 to 19 percent drop in energy output between 2031 and 2060.

If coal is going to adapt to people's needs, we may need to think outside the lump. Coal does not have to be used in its solid form. It can be converted into a cleaner-burning gas. Gasifying can be done above ground, but there are also underground gasification programs in several countries, including China, Canada, the United Kingdom, and the U.S. Coal is burned underground to convert it into a gas, and then it is collected through a hole. During the process, pollutants such as sulfur, mercury, and ash are largely left underground, while carbon dioxide emissions are captured. However, the problem of storing this carbon dioxide remains. Also, the area's geology must be just right to support underground gasification, so there are limited places where it can be done. It's also possible to turn coal into a liquid fuel to power cars or other vehicles. This has been done, but it's

Some coal-fueled power plants withdraw more than 50 million gallons (189 million l) of water per day.

a complex process that costs a lot and has historically been used only as a last resort. In recent years, though, China's largest coal-producing company has been working on improving the technology.

Over the last 20 years, talk of a hydrogen-based economy has increased. Hydrogen could power cars or other machines through systems called fuel cells. Hydrogen itself would not actually be the energy source. Instead, it would be manufactured by using another feedstock—a raw material—such as coal or natural gas, which both contain

hydrogen. However, "making" hydrogen is expensive and inefficient. A lot of energy contained in the feedstock is used up in the process of isolating the hydrogen. But it's a much cleaner option, and many researchers are enthusiastic about learning how to harvest hydrogen from the environment.

In the U.S. in 2012, the Environmental Protection Agency (EPA) proposed limits on the amount of carbon pollution that power plants may emit. The regulations meant that new coal-burning plants would be allowed to emit only about half the carbon dioxide

that most current plants produce. The EPA was also working on stiffer regulations for existing power plants. David Pumphrey, a co-director of the Center for Strategic and International Studies, says, "This is not a sudden death for the coal industry.... But it says the future of coal is limited and probably isn't going to grow more than it is now." Other countries were also passing tighter regulations about pollution toward the middle of the decade.

Scientists are racing to develop technologies to make coal a better option, but even if coal were squeaky clean, it still has one issue that can't be fixed: it's finite and unable to be renewed or expanded. While the world still has large deposits of coal, demand is increasing quickly. Each day adds more people to the planet, and each day, more of those people require more energy.

Coal will not be available to meet humans' energy needs forever. The first study of U.S. coal reserves, conducted in the early 1900s, predicted the country had enough coal to last 5,000 years. Now, many estimates say 250 years. But even that number is based on information that's 40 years old. In 2010, a Chinese study concluded the country had 62 years' worth of coal, but that number was calculated from the rate of demand for coal in 2009. Taking into account China's increasing use, and its ever-expanding population, it's possible the supply would last only 19 years. In 2011, a new stash of coal was found in China that potentially would extend the resource's life span, but people could not be sure.

Coal's current availability and relatively low price mean that it will likely fulfill much of the world's energy needs over the next 50 years. But already, shortages are happening in China, India, and other developing countries. And natural gas—which is cheaper and cleaner—is gaining ground. People once believed coal could last forever. But it's becoming clear that the end of forever is approaching sooner than we had thought.

Since the 1980s, the state of Wyoming has been the leading producer of U.S. coal.

CHAPTER FOUR

A DIRTY DEBATE

COAL ISN'T AN IDEAL SOURCE OF FUEL IN TERMS OF ENERGY EFFICIENCY OR EARTH'S WELL-BEING. But it's economical, and the mechanisms to mine and use it are already in place. While it may seem easy and cheap, its convenience still comes at a cost. It dirties the air, damages the land, and puts people in danger. So, is it worth it? American environmental author Jeff Goodell argues in his book *Big Coal* that coal has had its moment, and that it's time to move on. "Coal was supposed to be the engine of the industrial revolution, not the Internet revolution," he writes.

But Chinese energy expert Ming Sung counters such stances by saying, "People without a technical background think, 'Coal is dirty! It's bad.' But will you turn off your refrigerator for 30 years while we work on renewables? Turn off your computer?... Unless you will, you can't get rid of coal for decades."

The tug-of-war between the economy and the environment continues every day. Environmentalists talk about a "rooftop revolution." Instead of generating power at large facilities, they argue it could be made on a much smaller scale at individual homes or businesses. (The "rooftop" refers to solar panels on a roof.) Currently, electric power is produced at gigantic plants and distributed through a complex network. Power plants are coal's biggest customers, so coal companies want to keep the structure this way.

In 2012, more than 81 percent of U.S. coal supplied the country's power plants.

*Surface mining pits can sometimes be filled in
with vegetation, but scars remain.*

Some advocates for coal say that it is the best way to bring the
world more electricity. Billions of people have little or no access
to electric power. Studies show that increased access to electricity
improves lives. People who live in societies with reliable electricity
live longer, have better access to education, and earn more money.
Providing electricity—through coal-fired plants—could raise the
standard of living and comfort for a lot of people. In short, people
in the coal industry argue that coal is too useful to give up. They

say the solution is not to stop using it but to improve how it is used. Opponents say that coal is too dirty and dangerous to deserve a place in the world's energy mix.

There may be a future for cleaner coal, but history supports the case of environmentalists. Surface mining and mountaintop removal kill vegetation on the land. They spill toxins such as arsenic, cadmium, and selenium into the soil and water supply. Large swaths of land all around the globe—from America's Appalachian Mountains to the valleys of Wales in the United Kingdom—have been transformed from lush landscapes into dead, blackened deserts.

The anthracite coal continues to burn in Centralia, Pennsylvania, venting gases into the air.

Coal fires present yet another problem. Sometimes, underground coal mines catch fire, where they can burn for decades or even longer. In Centralia, Pennsylvania, a web of mines caught fire in 1962. They are still burning and could for another 250 years. Eventually, the land began to collapse, and by the early 1980s, residents had started to abandon the town. Only a handful of people remained by 2010. In China and India, thousands of coal fires dot the landscape. Because they originate underground, these fires are difficult—or sometimes impossible—to put out.

Although coal produces less carbon dioxide *overall* than other fossil fuels, it produces *more* in relation to the amount of energy it provides. In fact, coal burning produces about one-third of global carbon dioxide emissions. Coal-fired plants chug it into the air at alarming rates, and a warming planet is just one of the consequences. In a blow to the coal industry, the U.S. Supreme Court ruled in 2007 that carbon dioxide was dangerous enough to be considered a threat to public health and that it should be regulated by the government as such.

Carbon-capturing technology, though it exists, is often attached to a traditional coal plant, requiring more energy to operate it. That means more coal. Additionally, the systems in operation capture only about

Underground fires can spread to the surface, causing quick-moving brush or forest fires.

0.1 percent of total emissions. Building enough CCS systems would be an enormous undertaking that many experts doubt would prove worthwhile.

Some countries have regulations in place about the amount of pollutants and greenhouse gases that can be emitted by coal-fired plants. Environmentalists often object that these rules don't go far enough. For example, new standards in the U.S. apply to only new factories, not existing ones. For decades, coal companies have dodged regulations by upgrading old plants instead of building new ones. That way, they did not have to follow the stricter rules.

A system called "cap-and-trade" is at work in some places. Governments put a "cap" on how much pollution a coal company can produce. However, these companies can then "trade" with others in the industry. Companies that produce more than their allotted emissions can buy allowances from those that make less. While this regulates the overall amount of pollution, opponents say it discourages some companies from cleaning up their acts.

The human cost from coal is tremendous. Mining is one of the most dangerous jobs around. For deep mining, people have to venture thousands of feet underground. As

they dig into the earth, it becomes unstable. Sometimes mines collapse and trap or kill people. China has an especially bad safety record, losing about 5,000 miners to accidents every year. In addition, mining can release gases that can poison or kill someone.

The most widespread health problem for miners is breathing in coal dust. Miners are susceptible to getting black lung disease. Coal dust builds up in the lungs and eventually can cause death. In 1969, the U.S. Congress passed the Coal Mine Health and Safety Act to try to stem the tide of miners with black lung disease. While the numbers have improved, the American Lung Association still blames coal for the deaths of 24,000 Americans each year. The numbers are similar in Europe—and worse in China.

Yet coal remains capable of being economically successful. The coal industry points out that mining provides jobs and that coal is a vital part of the global economy. Australia, Indonesia, South Africa, Russia, and other countries all depend on coal exports. Most U.S. coal goes to **domestic** uses, but exports are increasing. The main importers are Japan, South Korea, Taiwan, Germany, and the United Kingdom. China and India currently rely mostly on domestic coal reserves as well. But

Willing workers are
scarce in some areas
of the mining industry.

35

they may turn to imports if prices rise and they cannot meet their demand with in-country supplies. Just the transportation involved in moving all this coal around is a huge industry. If it suddenly stopped, it could hurt the entire world's economy.

Energy security is another factor affecting the future use of coal. Many countries want to be self-sufficient when it comes to energy. That way, they do not have to depend on imports from other nations—which often involves negotiating for prices and supply. Using a domestic resource means that there is less chance of the price going up sharply or of being cut off from the supply entirely. If political relations between the importer and exporter become tense, having their own supplies gives each some independence. It also makes the resource cheaper to use, because there are lower transportation costs. Coal is widespread, relatively easy to access, and relatively inexpensive. It's no wonder that during the 19th century it became the world's dominant fuel and that it's managed to retain that status through the 20th and into the 21st centuries. Whether it should continue to stay on top is the big question. Coal companies say yes. Environmentalists say no. Governments and economists say both. For the next few decades, what will burn even hotter than coal will be the debate surrounding it.

Coal is shipped at all hours. As of 2012, Indonesia was the world's top exporter.

In 1306, the smoke from the coal fires of London was overpowering. English nobles, in town for a meeting of Parliament, protested the obnoxious smell. King Edward I responded by banning the burning of coal. Offenders faced fines, the destruction of their furnaces, or even execution. But wood was expensive, coal was cheap, and most citizens ignored the law. In 1952, a "black fog" of poisonous coal smoke settled over the city, trapped there for days by a layer of cold air. Thousands of people died. In 1956, Parliament passed a law limiting coal burning in the city limits. This time, it worked.

Not many people had porch lights in the late 18th century, but Scottish inventor William Murdoch helped change that. Murdoch, who had worked to develop a high-pressure steam engine with James Watt, began experimenting with heating coal to produce a gas in 1792. Then, he channeled this gas into a thin tube, where it could be set on fire and used as a light. Murdoch outfitted his home with gaslights, and he later used the technology to help illuminate Watt's factory, the Soho Foundry, in Birmingham, England. Gaslights became a common sight in homes and on streets in the 19th century.

London police tried to direct traffic before transportation came to a standstill in 1952 (left). Murdoch's gaslights have evolved with the widespread use of electricity (right).

Coal mining created jobs—but they weren't always good ones. In the 1600s, Scottish colliers (coal miners) were legally required to work in mines. Before and during the Industrial Revolution, working conditions in coal mines were often unspeakably bad. Hours were long. Spaces were cold, damp, and dark. Workers were exposed to poisonous chemicals and gases without proper protection. Mines flooded and collapsed, killing those trapped inside. Even children were forced to work in the mines. By the early 1800s, workers formed **labor unions** to fight for their rights. Over time, the unions gained power and were able to improve the lives of miners.

Why bother hauling coal to the surface just to make it into gas? Underground coal gasification has been a global effort for almost 150 years. British scientist William Siemens first suggested the idea in 1868. In 1913, Scottish chemist William Ramsay began building a UCG plant, but the effort stalled when World War I started in 1914. However, Russia stepped in to improve the technology in the 1920s, and European countries revived the effort after World War II ended in 1945. U.S. scientists joined the cause in the 1970s, Australia set up an experimental site in the late 1990s, and China had several projects underway in the 2010s.

Nineteenth-century miners used pickaxes and shovels to access much of the coal (left). Siemens's plan for coal gasification inspired further innovation (right).

In the 1920s, two German researchers, Franz Fischer and Hans Tropsch, devised a way to convert coal into liquid form. During World War II (1939–45), the process was used to change Germany's abundant coal reserves into fuel that could power cars and tanks. (Germany had no petroleum and couldn't buy it during the war.) South Africa also has been a heavy user of liquid coal. For decades, other countries refused to do business with South Africa because of the government system of **apartheid**. To help meet its energy needs, South Africa turned to converting its own coal reserves to liquid form.

Almost 5,000 miners reported to work one April day in 1942 at the Benxihu Colliery (coal mine) in China. A third of them never came home. An explosion of gas and coal dust killed many who were down in the mine. Then it got worse. At the time, Japan was at war with China and was occupying the country. To try to contain the fire, Japanese guards on the surface sealed the entrance to the mine, trapping the workers (mostly Chinese) underground. Some of the 1,500 miners who died burned to death, but many more suffocated when they could not escape.

Coal-fueled motorcars made their appearance during the World Wars, when gasoline was limited and expensive. Such vehicles stored fuel in a balloon on the roof (left).

Fish were dying. Trees were withering. Buildings were corroding. People's hair was turning green. In the 1960s and 1970s, something was very wrong with the environment. Scientists were scrambling to figure out what it was. The **culprit** turned out to be acid rain, which contained poisonous nitrogen oxides and sulfur dioxide. Acid rain had first been noticed in the 1850s, but it wasn't until 1962 that Swedish scientist Svante Odén showed that it came from industrial pollution such as burning coal. The problem spurred governments in the U.S. and Europe to regulate the amount of pollutants coal plants could emit.

In 2003, U.S. president George W. Bush approved a plan for the government to partner with private companies to build an environmentally friendly power plant called FutureGen. It would be a coal-burning power plant to make electricity as well as hydrogen that could be used as fuel. It would also use CCS technology to keep carbon emissions almost at zero. The project had many problems, and in 2008, the government backed out as it became too expensive. But in 2010, president Barack Obama revived the idea. Construction of FutureGen 2.0 was scheduled to start in 2013, with an operational date of 2017.

Forests and wildlife are devastated by acid rain (center), a side effect of air pollution. Conservationists work to raise awareness of the pollutant's danger to wildlife (right).

apartheid—a system or policy that separates or discriminates on the basis of race

Carboniferous period—a geologic period that occurred from about 360 million to 286 million years ago characterized by the evolution of trees with bark and shallow, warm seas that created swamps

culprit—a person or thing responsible for doing something

domestic—within any given nation; not involving other countries

geological—having to do with the study of rocks and the physical formation of the earth

global warming—the phenomenon of Earth's average temperatures increasing over time

granules—very small pieces, or grains

greenhouse gases—gases that build up in Earth's atmosphere and prevent the release of heat

Industrial Revolution—a period from the late 1700s through the 1800s in Europe and the U.S. marked by a shift from economies based on agriculture and handicraft to ones dominated by mechanized production in factories

infrastructure—the services and mechanisms used to support a society

labor unions—groups of workers who join together to gain political power

oxymoron—a phrase whose words appear to contradict one another

radar—a process of using radio waves to detect the distance and motion of other objects

react—when two or more substances chemically bind together to create a new substance

renewable—able to be replenished and used indefinitely

residue—part of a substance that is left behind after coming into contact with something else

seams—long, relatively thin underground layers, as of minerals or coal

sludge—a thick mixture of liquid and solid materials, usually as waste from an industrial process

Stone Age—a period of about 3.5 million years during which humans used stone to make tools, before the introduction of metalworking

turbine—a machine that is driven by water, steam, or a gas flowing through the blades of a wheel

Fallows, James. "Dirty Coal, Clean Future." *The Atlantic*, December 2010.

Freese, Barbara. *Coal: A Human History*. New York: Penguin, 2004.

"The Future is Black." *The Economist*, January 21, 2012.

Goodell, Jeff. *Big Coal: The Dirty Secret Behind America's Energy Future*. New York: Houghton Mifflin, 2006.

Graetz, Michael J. *The End of Energy: The Unmaking of America's Environment, Security, and Independence*. Cambridge: Massachusetts Institute of Technology, 2011.

Heinberg, Richard. *Blackout: Coal, Climate and the Last Energy Crisis*. Gabriola Island, B.C.: New Society Publishers, 2009.

"IEA Report Sees No Let-up in World's Appetite for Coal over Next 5 Years." *Medium-Term Coal Market Report 2011*. International Energy Agency, December 13, 2011.

Smil, Vaclav. *Energy Myths and Realities: Bringing Science to the Energy Policy Debate*. Washington, D.C.: American Enterprise Institute for Public Policy Research, 2010.

Energy Quest: The Energy Story

http://energyquest.ca.gov/story/index.html
Several forms of energy are explored on this site, tracking the history of their usage and the technologies employed in harvesting or creating them.

U.S. Energy Information Administration

http://www.eia.gov/kids/energy.cfm?page=coal_home-basics
This section of the U.S. Energy Information Administration's website provides information on how coal is mined and processed, where the resource is used, and its environmental impacts.

NOTE: *Every effort has been made to ensure that the websites listed above are suitable for children, that they have educational value, and that they contain no inappropriate material. However, because of the nature of the Internet, it is impossible to guarantee that these sites will remain active indefinitely or that their contents will not be altered.*

Chapman, Garry, and Gary Hodges. *Coal*. Mankato, Minn.: Smart Apple Media, 2011.

Gunderson, Jessica. *The Energy Dilemma*. Mankato, Minn.: Creative Education, 2011.

Morris, Neil. *The Energy Mix*. Mankato, Minn.: Smart Apple Media, 2010.

Rooney, Anne. *Reducing the Carbon Footprint*. Mankato, Minn.: Smart Apple Media, 2010.

Royston, Angela. *Sustainable Energy*. Mankato, Minn.: Arcturus, 2009.

Rutter, John. *Mining, Minerals, and Metals*. Mankato, Minn.: Smart Apple Media, 2010.

Solway, Andrew. *Climate Change*. Mankato, Minn.: Smart Apple Media, 2010.

HARNESSING ENERGY • HARNESSING ENERGY

Published by Creative Education
P.O. Box 227, Mankato, Minnesota 56002
Creative Education is an imprint of The Creative Company
www.thecreativecompany.us

Design and production by The Design Lab
Art direction by Rita Marshall
Printed in the United States of America

Photographs by Alamy (Bernhard Classen, Cultura Creative, epa european
pressphoto agency b.v.), Corbis (Bettmann, Gary Fiegehen/All Canada Photos,
Hulton-Deutsch Collection, Frances Benjamin Johnston, Leif Skoogfors), Dreamstime
(Aniuszka, Tomasz Bidermann, Linda Bair, Emi Cristea, Jaroslaw Janczuk, Jarp3,
Alexey Kustov, Malajscy, Joseph Mercier, Nicku, Samrat35, David M. Schrader,
Threeart), Getty Images (Science & Society Picture Library/SSPL), Shutterstock
(Antonio Abrignani, abutyrin, Sissy Borbely, Danicek, Morphart Creation, Nneirda,
s_oleg, spirit of america, Aleksey Stemmer, Kuttelvaserova Stuchelova, Triff)

Library of Congress Cataloging-in-Publication Data
Bailey, Diane.
Coal power / Diane Bailey.
p. cm. — (Harnessing energy)
Includes bibliographical references and index.
Summary: An examination of the ways in which coal has historically been
used as an energy source and how current and future energy demands
are changing its technical applications and efficiency levels.
ISBN 978-1-60818-408-8
1. Coal—Juvenile literature. 2. Coal mines and mining—Juvenile literature. I. Title.

TP325.B227 2014
622'.334—dc23   2013035752

CCSS: RI.5.1, 2, 3, 4, 8, 9

First Edition
9 8 7 6 5 4 3 2 1